It's a
Mammal!

By Sharon Stewart

CELEBRATION PRESS

Pearson Learning Group

Contents

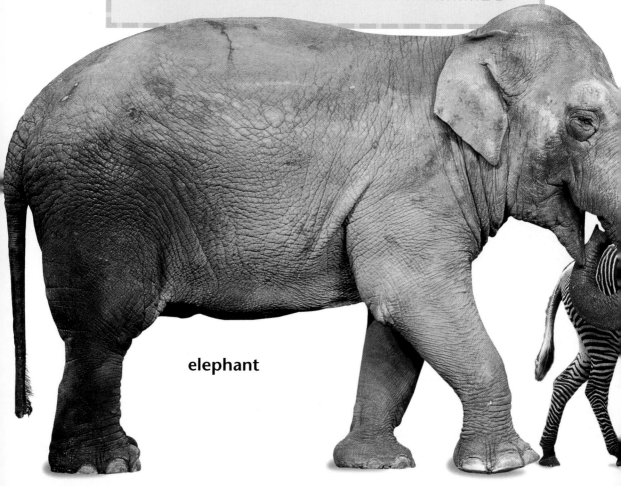

elephant

Many Animals

A cow munches on hay. A koala lives in a tree. A bat flies through the dark. A dog chases after a ball. It's clear that these animals are very different. Yet in one way they are alike. They are all mammals. Guess what? You're a mammal, too.

There are millions of species, or kinds of animals. There are about 4,000 species of mammals. Why are these animals called mammals? What makes them different from birds or reptiles?

Mammals come in all shapes and sizes, from huge elephants to tiny mice.

zebra

human

bat

dog

fox

chinchilla

mouse

What Is a Mammal?

Mammals have certain things in common. Mammal mothers produce milk for their babies to drink. Most mammals have fur, or hair, to keep them warm. They are also **warmblooded**. This means that their body temperature does not depend on the temperature outside. Mammals also have a skeleton that is held together by a backbone.

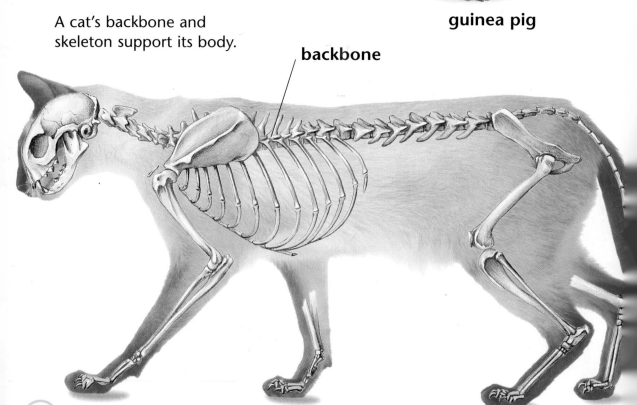

guinea pig

A cat's backbone and skeleton support its body.

backbone

Most mammals give birth to their babies. However, the duck-billed platypus (PLAT-ih-puss) and the echidna (eh-KIHD-nuh) lay eggs instead. In this way, these mammals are like reptiles.

Most mammal babies are fully formed when they are born. **Marsupials**, like the wallaby, are different. They are born when they are still tiny and only partly formed. They do most of their growing inside a warm pouch on their mother's belly.

echidna

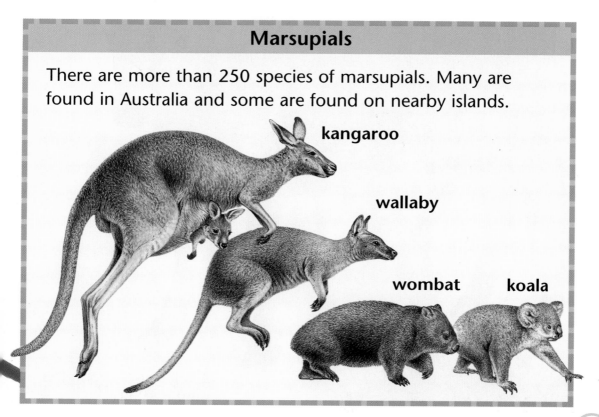

Marsupials

There are more than 250 species of marsupials. Many are found in Australia and some are found on nearby islands.

kangaroo

wallaby

wombat

koala

Baby Mammals

Most baby mammals need their mothers' milk to live. In fact, their mothers' milk is the only food very young mammals eat. It is full of **nutrients** to help them grow. It also contains the water they need to survive.

Reptiles, such as snakes and turtles, cannot make milk. Baby reptiles take care of themselves almost from birth. Baby mammals, however, need their parents.

A calf grows strong from its mother's milk.

A mother bear takes her cubs fishing.

Mammal parents take care of their young. They feed them and protect them from harm. Mammal parents play with their young and teach them how to behave. Lions teach their cubs how to hunt and protect themselves. Horses teach their foals how to run. Mammal parents care for their babies until the babies are old enough to take care of themselves.

Keeping Warm

Many mammals have furry coats to help keep their bodies at the right temperature. Some have two coats of fur to trap the heat. The Arctic musk ox has short wool under its long hair.

Arctic musk ox

Many water mammals don't have furry coats like land mammals. Instead, some water mammals, such as walruses, have blubber. Blubber is a layer of fat under the skin. It keeps these mammals warm.

walrus

Some mammals, such as the dormouse, woodchuck, and some bats, **hibernate** during the cold winter. First, they eat to fatten themselves up. When the cold weather comes, they fall into a sleeplike state.

They do not need much energy, so hibernating mammals usually do not eat. Their fat gives them enough energy and keeps them warm. Then, when spring comes and the weather is warmer, they wake up.

dormouse

Can you see the hibernating dormouse?

Where Mammals Live

Mammals live in many different places, or **habitats**. They live in grasslands and in deserts, on Arctic shores and in rain forests. Their bodies have **adapted** to survive many conditions.

Camels have adapted to live in the hot, dry desert where there is little food or water. They get energy from a fatty substance stored inside their humps. Their thick foot pads protect them from the hot sand.

In sandstorms, camels close their nostrils and keep out sand with their long double eyelashes.

The polar bear's coat blends into the snow.

Polar bears are well adapted to their cold Arctic habitat. Their fur is made of hollow hairs that capture the heat of the sun. Their tough, dark skin takes in much of this warmth. They also have a thick layer of fat under their skin. Their big paws have hair on the bottom to grip the slippery ice. They have adapted to the icy Arctic waters, and they are excellent swimmers.

Endangered Mammals

Mammals, like all animals, depend on their habitats for survival. All over the world, mammals are losing their habitats and food sources. Many mammals live in areas where humans are taking over land. Animals cannot adapt to this change.

Some animals may soon become **extinct**. This means that all of that kind of animal die out. Animals that may become extinct are called **endangered** animals. More mammals are endangered than any other kind of animal.

The giant panda, found in China, is endangered.

Some Endangered Species

black rhinoceros

- **kind of habitat:** grassland and open woodland

- **location:** parts of central and southern Africa

tiger

- **kind of habitat:** tropical forest and **deciduous forest**

- **location:** parts of southern and eastern Asia

woodland caribou

- **kind of habitat:** **coniferous forest** and tundra

- **location:** parts of northern Canada

gray wolf

- **kind of habitat:** coniferous forest, tundra, and mountains

- **location:** parts of North America, Europe, and Siberia

Mammals on the Move

Most mammals move around on four legs. They run, walk, or trot. Some jump and leap, and others swim and fly. Some two-legged mammals, like humans, walk, run, or jump.

Mammals That Jump

Australia's kangaroos are possibly the most famous jumping mammals. They hop along by pushing off the ground with their large feet and powerful back legs. Believe it or not, red kangaroos can leap more than 25 feet in a single bound. That's more than four times as far as they are tall!

Red Kangaroo

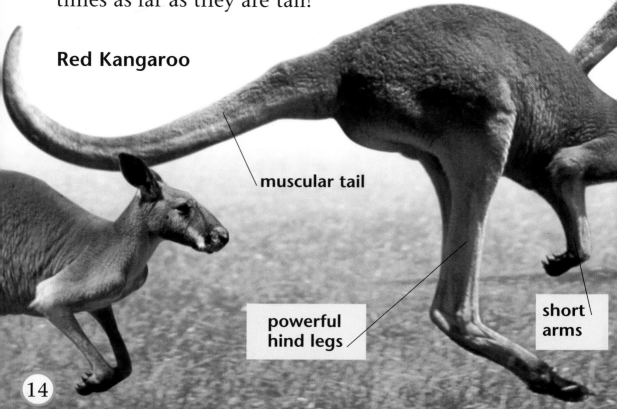

muscular tail

powerful hind legs

short arms

Australia's brush-tailed rock wallabies are also great jumpers. Wallabies are small- to medium-sized mammals in the kangaroo family. Brush-tailed rock wallabies have padded hind feet to help them grip the rocky cliffs on which they live. They can jump about 13 feet high.

brush-tailed rock wallaby

Other Mammals That Jump

impala

antelope

rabbit

jerboa

Mammals That Fly

Bats are the only mammals that can fly. Most bats have sharp teeth and big ears. All bats have wings made of leathery skin. This skin is stretched over their arm and finger bones. Bats' wings vary in size. Some bats have wingspans of more than 5 feet. Others have wingspans of only 6 inches.

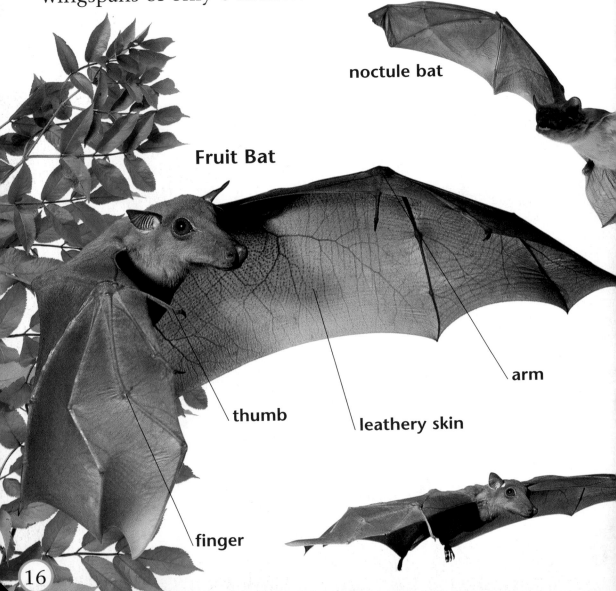

noctule bat

Fruit Bat

arm

thumb

leathery skin

finger

Bats often roost in caves during the day and come out at night.

Some bats fly as high as 10,000 feet as they move from place to place. As they fly around, they often scatter seeds and **pollinate** plants. Bats fly mostly at night. This is because they are **nocturnal** mammals. They leave their homes at night to find food such as fruit, insects, or small animals. A bat can eat up to 3,000 insects in one night!

Bats can see, but some also use **echolocation** to fly and hunt. Their high-pitched squeaks bounce off objects and echo back to them. This tells them where things are.

This long-eared bat has caught a moth.

Mammals That Swim

Mammals that live in the water, such as whales, have bodies that are shaped for swimming. Their skin is smooth, but like other mammals, whales have some hair. Instead of front legs, whales have flippers. Unlike fish, whales cannot breathe underwater. They must swim to the surface for air.

There are two kinds of whales: toothed whales and toothless whales. The biggest whales are toothless whales. They can grow to be more than 100 feet long and weigh nearly 150 tons.

The toothless whale family includes the humpback whale.

Many dolphins can swim
about 25 miles per hour.

Toothed whales, such as dolphins, hunt for food like fish and squid. The bottlenose dolphin is the most common type.

Walruses, seals, and sea lions are water mammals, like whales. Unlike whales, they have four flippers, one pair in the front and one pair at the back. Most of their lives are spent in water. At least once a year, they settle on beaches or sea ice. There, they give birth to their babies.

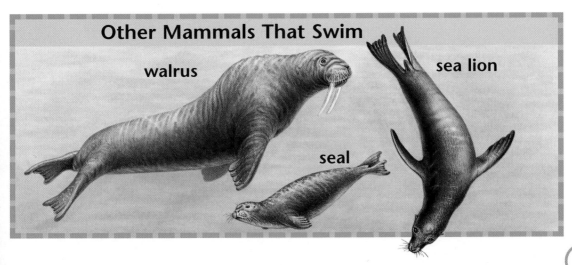

Other Mammals That Swim

walrus

sea lion

seal

Mammal Senses

Most mammals, like people, have five senses. The five senses are sight, sound, smell, taste, and touch. Many animals' senses are better than humans'.

Bush babies, animals similar to monkeys, see and hear far better than humans. At night their huge eyes pick up the faintest light. Their large ears swivel to track flying insects. Then they swing out like acrobats to snatch the insects in midair.

Rabbits are terrific tasters because they have 17,000 taste buds! That's 7,000 more than humans have.

The bush baby's large eyes help it see at night.

The hedgehog's special talent is sniffing. Its moist, twitchy nose can find worms about an inch below the ground. Its nose helps the hedgehog track down spiders, snakes, and mice. Hedgehogs find each other using scent trails.

Touch is important to monkeys. They touch or kiss when they meet. They spend hours grooming each other. Grooming seems to relax them and strengthen friendships.

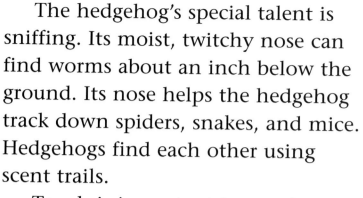

A hedgehog has poor sight but can smell very well.

One baboon is grooming another.

Amazing Mammals

Whether they run, hop, swim, or fly, mammals are amazing. Take a look at how different these mammals are.

The slowest mammal is the sloth. It moves only about 6 to 8 feet per minute.

The koala is the sleepiest mammal. It naps for up to 22 out of 24 hours each day.

The fastest land mammal is the cheetah. For a short distance, it can run at 60 miles per hour.

Glossary

adapted — changed to survive in a particular habitat

coniferous forest — a forest made up mostly of trees with needle-like leaves that stay green all year

deciduous forest — a forest made up mostly of trees that lose and regrow their leaves each year

echolocation — using echoes to locate objects

endangered — in danger of becoming extinct

extinct — this type of animal is no longer living

habitats — places where plants and animals live

hibernate — to go into a long, deep sleep, usually in winter

marsupials — mammals that carry their young in a pouch on their body

nocturnal — active at night

nutrients — substances that living things need to grow and be healthy

pollinate — to place pollen on a flower

warmblooded — having a body temperature that does not depend on the temperature outside

Index

The giraffe is the world's tallest mammal. It can be 18 feet tall. That's as tall as a second-story window!